IRIS
folding
with envelopes

**Maruscha Gaasenbeek
and Tine Beauveser**

FORTE PUBLISHERS

Contents

© 2001 Forte Uitgevers, Utrecht
© 2002 for the translation by the
publisher
Original title: *Irisvouwen met
enveloppen*

ISBN 90 5877 204 7

This is a publication from
Forte Publishers
Boothstraat 1c
3512 BT Utrecht
The Netherlands

Publisher: Marianne Perlot
Editor: Hanny Vlaar
Photography: Fotografie Gerhard
Witteveen, Apeldoorn, the Netherlands
Digital image editing: Marjan Huiskamp

Preface

There is something new under the sun: IRIS folding with envelopes!
Have you ever noticed the attractive colours and patterns on the inside
of envelopes? By cutting these envelopes into strips, folding them and
then sticking them on a card in a special way, you can create fantas-
tic greetings cards. What kind of envelopes, you may wonder. Well,
envelopes from your bank or insurance company, from the company
where your neighbour works or your friend's local council, from
your energy company or your children's school. There are so many
possibilities!
Stop throwing away used envelopes. Save them and swap them
with other IRIS folders. You will be amazed by all
the attractive patterns you receive. From now on, all post will be welcome.
You will even be pleased to receive an envelope from the tax department.
OK, we hear you say, but what is the iris? Colourful strips of paper which fill up the pattern from
the outside to the inside and join in the middle, just as the iris of your eye encloses the pupil.
But that's enough talking. Let's get started. Clear a space in your work corner, because the collect-
ing, folding and sticking is addictive! You will constantly discover more attractive envelopes which
you can use to make new combinations. The patterns in this book are suitable for making
cards for men. Each model is so much fun to make, that it is almost impossible to stop. You are
really going to enjoy yourself.
We wish you lots of fun with IRIS folding!

Thanks:
Wil Noback, for the rotating triangle.
Family, friends and acquaintances for saving the envelopes. Keep up the good work!

Techniques

The starting point for IRIS folding is the pattern. Cut the outer shape of the pattern out of the card and then fill the hole from the outside to the inside with folded strips of used envelopes. You work on the inside of the card, so that you work, in fact, on a mirror image. When you have finished, you cover the side you have been working on with a smaller card. For a triangular pattern, select three different envelopes where the patterns and colours combine nicely with each other. Cut all the envelopes into strips in the same way, for example, from top to bottom. Depending on the pattern, you will need between four and seven strips. First, you need to fold the strips down and sort them into each different type of envelope. Next, you cover each section in turn by following the numbers (1, 2, 3, 4, 5, etc.). Lay the strip on the section with the fold facing towards the middle of the pattern and then stick them on the left-hand and right-hand sides of the card using adhesive tape. Finally, use an attractive piece of holographic paper to cover the hole in the middle. Avoid colour differences by using only one envelope for the same design.

The BASIC TRIANGLE
(see card 1 in chapter 1)
The most important thing is to start with the basic triangle, because from this, you will learn the unique folding and sticking technique needed for all the patterns.

The cards in this book get increasingly more difficult. Therefore, start at the beginning. You will notice that you quickly get used to the technique of IRIS folding.

Preparation
1 Take a white card (14.8 x 21 cm). Fold it double and lay it down with the inside facing towards you.

2 Draw pencil lines on the left-hand side of the card halfway along the width and length. These lines will help you determine the place for your pattern.

3 Copy the basic triangle pattern 1A from this book

4 Place this model on the left-hand side of the card on the lines which you drew earlier.

5 Use a pin to prick through the pattern and the card in the three corners of the pattern.

6 Remove the pattern and carefully cut the triangle out of the card.

7 Tape the basic triangle pattern 1A to your cutting mat.

8 Place the card on top with the hole exactly over the pattern (you should be looking at the inside of the card) and stick the top and bottom edges to your cutting mat using a couple of pieces of masking tape.

1 The choice of colours: the inside of different envelopes.

2 Copy the pattern onto the left-hand inside of the card. Cut out the parts of the boat.

3 Cut the envelopes into strips and fold them double. Stick the pattern to your cutting mat and place the card on top of it.

4 Place the strips from bottom to top in colours A, B and C over the spinnaker and stick down the left-hand and right-hand sides using adhesive tape.

9   Choose three envelopes with different patterns. Three different blue envelopes have been used for card 1 in chapter 1.

10 Cut 2 cm wide strips from these envelopes (either lengthways or widthways) and make separate piles of colour A, colour B and colour C.

11 Fold each strip down (approximately 7 mm) along the entire length with the nice side facing outwards.

IRIS folding

12 Take a folded strip of colour A and place this over section 1 of the pattern with the folded side facing towards the middle. Allow 1 cm to stick out on the left-hand and right-hand sides and cut off the rest.

13 Stick the strip to the card on the left-hand and right-hand sides using a small piece of adhesive tape, but remain at least 0.5 cm from the side of the card.

14 Take a strip of colour B and place it on section 2 of the pattern. Also tape this to the left-hand and right-hand sides of the card.

15 Take a strip of colour C. Place this on section 3 and stick it into place.

16 You have now gone all the way around. Start again with colour A on section 4, colour B on section 5 and colour C on section 6.

Continue going around the card.

The strips on sections 1, 4, 7, 10 and 13 of this pattern are all of colour A. The strips on sections 2, 5, 8, 11 and 14 are all of colour B. The strips on sections 3, 6, 9, 12 and 15 are all of colour C.

Finishing

After section 15, carefully remove the card and look at what you have made. Stick a single piece of silver holographic paper in the middle on the back of the card. Take a white card (14.6 x 10.3 cm) and stick small pieces of double-sided adhesive tape around the edge. Remove the protective layer from the tape and stick the card against the back of the pattern to cover everything nicely. Do not use glue, because all the paper strips place pressure on the card. You can use punches, figure scissors, stickers and card of different colours to add extra finishing touches to the card. To cut the card using figure scissors, a pencil line is drawn on the back of the card 0.5 cm from the edge. Cut along the line using the teeth of the scissors. Fold the cut part backwards and carefully place the teeth of the scissors in the pattern which has already been cut out. This will create a border which continues in one continuous line.

Materials

To make the cards:

- ❏ Card
- ❏ Punched cards
- ❏ Cutting knife
- ❏ Cutting mat
- ❏ Pencil
- ❏ Ruler with a metal cutting edge
- ❏ Adhesive tape
- ❏ Double-sided adhesive tape
- ❏ Masking tape
- ❏ Various punches (Tom Tas)
- ❏ Scissors
- ❏ Figure scissors (Fiskars)
- ❏ Ridge master
- ❏ Fine-liners
- ❏ Gel pens
- ❏ Photo glue
- ❏ Stickers
- ❏ Embossing pen
- ❏ Embossing templates
- ❏ Light box

For the IRIS folding:

Used envelopes from:
- ❏ Banks
- ❏ Insurance companies
- ❏ Local councils
- ❏ Companies
- ❏ Institutions
- ❏ Schools
- ❏ Trade unions
- ❏ Societies
- ❏ Advertisements

The middle of the card:

- ❏ Silver or gold holographic paper
- ❏ Shiny origami paper

The patterns:

All the patterns are given in this book. Copy them using a light box. The straight lines make the patterns easy to cut out of card. Special, punched cards are available for the sailboat, the teapot, the small butterflies and the windmill.

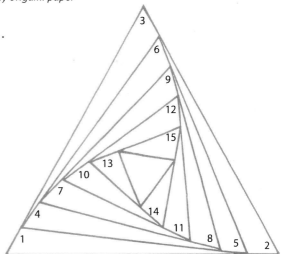

pattern 1A

Triangles

This basic pattern will teach you the unique method of folding and sticking used for IRIS folding.

For all the cards, follow the instructions given for the basic triangle (see Techniques).

Card 1

Card: white (14.8 x 21 cm and 14.6 x 10.3 cm)
• Pattern 1A • 2 cm wide strips from 3 different blue envelopes • Butterfly punch
Punch out four butterflies. Stick two on the card using glue.
Stick the bodies of the other butterflies on the butterflies already stuck on the card and fold the wings upwards. Decorate the card using an ivy embossing stencil.

Card 2

Card: dark blue (14.8 x 21 cm), grey (Papicolor no. 20) (14.4 x 10 cm) and light lavender (Papicolor no. 21) (14.2 x 9.7 cm) • Pattern 1A

2.

7.

3.

4.

• 2 cm wide strips from 3 different pink/purple
envelopes • Text sticker • Corner punch •
Silver holographic paper
Cut the triangle out of the light lavender card
and punch out the corners. After completing
the IRIS folding, stick the cards on each other,
in ascending order of size, using double-sided
adhesive tape.

Card 3

*Card: lavender blue (Papicolor no. 31) (14.8 x
21 cm) and white (14.8 x 10.5 cm) • Pattern 1A •
2 cm wide strips from 3 different blue envelopes
• Gold holographic paper • Butterfly punch •
Figure scissors • Bee stamp • Line stickers
• Text sticker*
Cut around the edge of the white card using the
figure scissors. Stick the white card on the blue
card and decorate it with butterflies, stamps,
line stickers and a text sticker.

Card 4

*Card: white (14.8 x 21 cm and 14.8 x 10.5 cm)
• Pattern 1B • 2 cm wide strips from 3 different
blue envelopes • Silver holographic paper •
Figure scissors • Text sticker • Line stickers and
corner stickers*
Fold the card double and cut a strip off the
right-hand side using figure scissors. Determine
the position for the triangle and follow the
instructions given for the basic triangle. Finish
the card with a text sticker, corner stickers and
line stickers.

Card 5

Card: grey (14.8 x 21 cm), red (14.4 x 10.1 cm)
and white (14 x 9.7 cm) • Pattern 1B • 2 cm
wide strips from 3 different red, purple and
black-and-white envelopes • Corner punch
• Origami paper
Punch out the corners of the white card.

Card 6

Card: grey (Papicolor no. 21) (14.8 x 21 cm),
red (14.2 x 10.3 cm) and blue (13.8 x 10.3 cm)
• Pattern 1B • 2 cm wide strips from 3 different
red, purple and black-and-white envelopes •
Figure scissors • Text sticker • Gold holographic
paper
Cut around the edge of the blue card using
the figure scissors.

Card 7

Card: dark blue (Papicolor no. 41)
(26.6 x 13.3 cm), lilac (12.3 x
12.3 cm) and white (12.1 x 12.1 cm)
• Pattern 1A • 2 cm wide strips
from 3 different purple/pink
envelopes • Line stickers •
Text stickers • Gold holographic paper
Punch out the corners
of the white card.

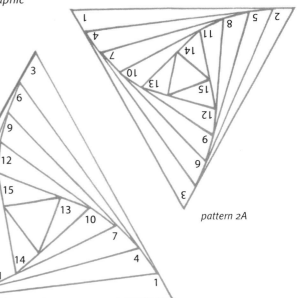

pattern 2A

pattern 1B

Playing with triangles

Turn them to the left and right.

Or have them standing

straight up or upside down!

Card 1

Card: blue (14.8 x 21 cm and 14.6 x 10.3 cm) • Pattern 2A • 2 cm wide strips from three different blue/grey envelopes • Silver holographic paper

Cut the triangles out of the left-hand side of the card. Stick the strips on the card in order, i.e. 1, 2, 3, etc. Cover the middle with holographic paper. Cut 0.4 cm wide strips from one of the envelopes and stick them on the card parallel to the triangles, as shown in the photograph.

Card 2

Card: grey (14.8 x 21 cm) and white (14.5 x 9.6 cm) • Pattern 2B • 2 cm wide strips from 3 different envelopes with a grey pattern • Stickers • Silver holographic paper

Cut the diamond shape of pattern 2B out of the white card. First, make a starting strip using a strip of colour A (8 x 2 cm). Fold this strip to a size of 8 x 0.8 cm by folding over both edges. Stick the starting strip on the card according to the pattern and follow the rest of the instructions given for the basic triangle. When finished, stick it on grey card and stick line stickers on the card which go from the middle to the edge of the card. Decorate the card using a text sticker.

Card 3

Card: white (14.8 x 21 cm and 14.6 x 10.3 cm) • Pattern 2A • 2 cm wide strips from 3 different blue envelopes • Blue origami paper

Follow the instructions given for card 1. Cut 0.4 cm wide strips of colour C and stick them on the card, as shown in the photograph.

starting strip (colour a, same as 1, 4, 7 ect.)

pattern 2B

Card 4

Card: dark blue (14.8 x 21 cm and 14.8 x 9.5 cm) • Pattern 2C • 2 cm wide strips from 3 different blue envelopes • Silver holographic paper

Cut the diamond shape out of the smallest card. Start with the starting strip, as explained for pattern 2B, and follow the rest of the instructions given for the basic triangle. To finish the card, cut two strips of colour A (14.8 x 1 cm) and stick them on the back of the card on the left-hand and right-hand sides so that 1 mm is visible on the front of the card. Stick all of this on the double card.

pattern 2C

Card 5

Card: dark blue (14.8 x 21 cm) and white (13.8 x 10 cm) • Sheet of envelope paper (colour A) (14.6 x 10.3 cm) • Pattern 2B • 2 cm wide strips from 3 different grey/blue envelopes • Corner punch • Text sticker • Silver holographic paper

Cut the diamond shape out of the white card and punch out the corners. Make a starting strip of colour A as described for card 2 and follow the instructions given for the basic triangle. Stick the white card on the sheet of envelope paper and stick this on the dark blue card. Decorate the card using a text sticker.

Card 6

Card: white (14.8 x 21 cm and 14.6 x 10.3 cm) • Pattern 2B • 2 cm wide strips from 3 different blue envelopes • Stickers • Corner scissors • Silver holographic paper

Start with a starting strip of colour A. Follow the instructions given for card 1. Stick the covering card against the back of the pattern to cover it over. Cut off two corners of the top card using the corner scissors and stick two corner stickers on the bottom card. Decorate the card using border stickers and a text sticker.

Card 7

Card: red (14.8 x 21 cm) and white (14.6 x 9.6 cm) • Pattern 2B • 2 cm wide strips from 2 different grey envelopes and a red envelope • Stickers • Corner punch • Silver holographic paper

Punch out the corners of the white card. The starting strip of colour A is the start of two IRIS folding triangles. Stick the finished IRIS folding card on the red card. Finish the card with line stickers and a text sticker.

Diagram labels (diamond): 3, 6, 9, 12, 15, 13, 10, 7, 4, 14, 11, 1, 2, 5, 8 — starting strip (colour a) — 1, 4, 7, 10, 13, 15, 14, 11, 8, 5, 2, 12, 9, 6, 3

Boats

A suitable card for a wedding,

a long holiday or a new job.

All the cards are made according to the instructions given for card 1.

Card 1

Card: white (14.8 x 21 cm and 14.6 x 10.3 cm) • Pattern 3A • 2 cm and 3 cm wide strips from three different blue envelopes • Stickers • Silver holographic paper
Cut out the boat as described in Techniques. Cover the hull with a 2 cm wide strip of colour C which has not been folded. Fold the 3 cm wide strips down and use them to cover the spinnaker. Follow the instructions given for the basic triangle. Decorate the card using line stickers and a text sticker.

Card 2

Card: light blue (Papicolor no. 02) (14.8 x 21 cm) and dark blue (Papicolor no. 41) (14.8 x 10.5 cm) • Pattern 3B • 2 cm and 3 cm wide strips from dark blue, white and blue, and sea green and white envelopes
• *Silver holographic paper • Text sticker • Figure scissors*
Cut around the edge of the dark blue card using the figure scissors. Stick the darker card on the double card and stick a text sticker on it.

Card 3

Card: blue (Papicolor no. 06) (14.8 x 21 cm) and white (14.8 x 10.5 cm) • Pattern 3A • 2 cm and 3 cm wide strips from three different blue envelopes • Blue/green origami paper • Figure scissors
Cut around the edge of the white card using the figure scissors. Stick the white card on the blue card.

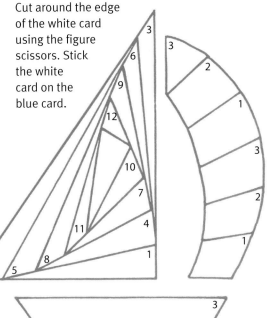

pattern 3B

Card 4

Card: white (14.8 x 21 cm and 14.6 x 10.3 cm)
• Pattern 3A • 2 cm and 3 cm wide strips from
3 different blue envelopes • Silver holographic
paper • Ridge master • Gel pen • Sticker
For this card, the boat sails along the longer
side of the card. Run the bottom corners
through the ridge master. Decorate the card
using the gel pens. Stick the covering card
against the inside of the card.

Card 5

Card: blue (Papicolor no. 6) (14.8 x 21 cm and
14.6 x 10.3 cm) • Pattern 3A • 2 cm and 3 cm
wide strips from 3 different blue envelopes
• Silver holographic paper
Cover the hull (colour C) and the spinnaker
(colour A) with a piece of envelope paper which
has not been folded. Cut out waves and birds in
colour C and stick them on the card.

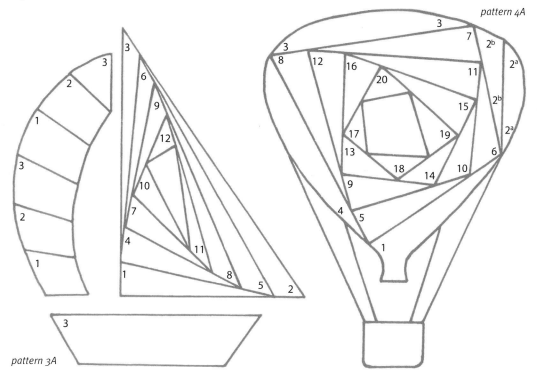

pattern 4A

pattern 3A

Balloons and kites

Go flying!

The balloons are made according to the instructions given for card 1. The kites are made according to the instructions given for card 2.

Card 1

Card: green (14.8 x 21 cm) and white (13.7 x 9.6 cm) • Sheet of envelope paper (14.3 x 10 cm) • Pattern 4A • 2 cm wide strips from 4 different green envelopes • Two 4 cm wide strips of colour A for sections 1 and 5 • Silver holographic paper • Black fine-liner • Text sticker

Punch out the corners of the white card using a corner punch. Draw the outer lines of the balloon and the basket on the white card and cut out both shapes (note: not the ropes!). Cover the basket with a piece of unfolded envelope paper in the colour of your choice. Follow the instructions given for the basic triangle. Draw the ropes with a fine-liner and draw speed lines. Stick the white card on the sheet of envelope paper and then stick everything on the green card.

Card 2

Card: light blue (Papicolor no. 19) (14.8 x 21 cm) and blue (Papicolor no 31) (14 x 9.8 cm) • Pattern 4B • Butterfly corner punch • 3 cm wide strips from 4 different blue and dark blue envelopes • Silver holographic paper

Punch butterflies in the corners of the blue card. Cut out the kite and fill it with the strips of envelope paper. Make a tail for the kite using bows and a piece of string.

Card 3

Card: blue (Papicolor no. 42) (14.8 x 21 cm and 14.6 x 10.3 cm) • Pattern 4A • 2 cm wide strips from 4 different blue envelopes • Two 4 cm wide strips of colour A for sections 1 and 5 • Silver holographic paper

Card 4

Card: green (Papicolor no. 18) (14.8 x 21 cm) and rainbow green (14.4 x 10.2 cm) • Sheet of envelope paper (14.4 x 10.2 cm) in colour D • Pattern 4B • 4 cm wide strips from 4 different green envelopes • Silver holographic paper • Figure scissors • Green thread

Cut around the edge of the rainbow card using the figure scissors. Decorate the card with some thread. Stick the card on the sheet of envelope paper and then stick everything on the green card.

Card 5

Card: brick red (Papicolor no. 33) (14.8 x 21 cm) and rainbow pink (13.8 x 9.4 cm) • Pattern 4B • Heart corner punch • 4 cm wide strips from 4 different beige/pink envelopes • Gold holographic paper
Punch out the corners.

Card 6

Card: brown (Papicolor no. 39) (14.8 x 21 cm) and cream (14.2 x 10.2 cm) • Pattern 4A • 2 cm wide strips from 4 different red/bruin envelopes • Two 4 cm wide strips of colour A • Gold holographic paper • Corner punch
Punch out the corners.

Card 7

Card: light brown (14.8 x 21 cm) and beige (Papicolor no. 29) (14 x 10 cm) • Sheet of orange envelope paper (14 x 10 cm) • Pattern 4A • 2 cm wide strips from 4 different brown/orange/yellow envelopes • Two 4 cm wide strips of colour A • Gold holographic paper • Figure scissors • Sticker
Cut around the edge of the beige card using the figure scissors.

Card 8

Card: dark red (Papicolor no. 43) (14.8 x 21 cm) and cream (13.8 x 9.6 cm) • Pattern 4A • 2 cm wide strips from 4 different red/pink envelopes • Two 4 cm wide strips of colour A • Gold-and-red holographic paper • Heart corner punch
Punch out the corners.

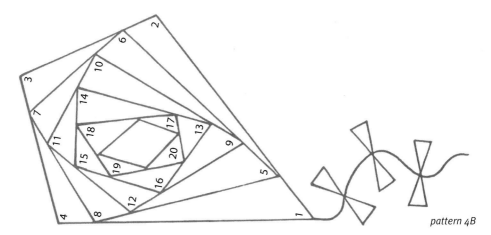

pattern 4B

Tea pots

For this model, you will not need 3 or 4, but 5 different envelopes which match and contrast each other nicely.

All the cards are made according to the instructions given for card 1.

Card 1

Card: ecru (Papicolor no. 03) (13.3 x 26.6 cm) and brown (Papicolor no. 39) (12 x 12 cm) • Pattern 5 • 2 cm wide strips from 5 different beige envelopes • Gold holographic paper • Cloud corner punch

Punch out the corners of the brown card. Cut out the pot (not the lid, the spout or the handle). Fill the pot with the strips as described for the basic triangle. Cut out the lid, the spout and the handle from envelope paper (colour B) and stick them around the pot on the front of the card.

1.

3.

2.

4.

Card 2
Card: green (Papicolor no. 18) (13.3 x 26.6 cm)
and white (Papicolor no. 30) (12.4 x 12.4 cm)
• Pattern 5 • 2 cm wide strips from 5 different
green envelopes • Silver holographic paper •
Lily corner punch
Punch out the corners of the white card.

Card 3
Card: cloudy blue-grey (Papicolor no. 52)
(13.3 x 26.6 cm) and dark blue (Papicolor no. 41)
(12.6 x 12.6 cm) • Pattern 5 • 2 cm wide strips
from 5 different grey envelopes • Silver holographic paper.

Card 4
Card: brown (Papicolor no. 39) (13.3 x 26.6 cm)
and cream (Papicolor no. 29) (12 x 12 cm) •
Pattern 5 • 2 cm wide strips from 5 different
beige/brown/red envelopes • Silver holographic
paper • Heart corner punch
Punch out the corners of the cream card.

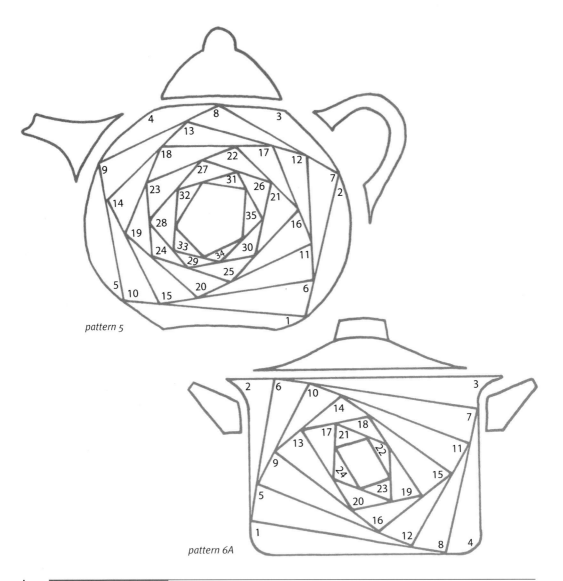

pattern 5

pattern 6A

Pots and pans

An invitation to or a thank you for

a dinner or an enjoyable evening.

Card 1

Card: dark blue (14.8 x 21 cm) and rainbow blue (14 x 9.6 cm) • Pattern 6A • 2.5 cm strips from 4 different blue envelopes • Silver holographic paper • Heart corner punch

Cut out the pan (not the lid or the handles) from the rainbow card. Fill the hole with the strips of envelope paper. Turn the card over. Cut out the lid and the handles from envelope paper (colour C) and stick them on the card.

Card 2

Card: white (14.8 x 21 cm and 12.8 x 9.4 cm) • Sheet of envelope paper in colour B (14 x 9.8 cm) • Pattern 6A • 2.5 cm wide strips from 4 different envelopes • Gold holographic paper • Corner punch • Linda Design embossing stencil

Cut the pan out of a landscape-shape card. Follow the instructions given for card 1.

Card 3

Card: brick red (Papicolor no. 35) (14.8 x 21 cm)

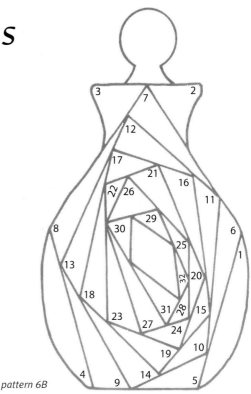

pattern 6B

and white (14.8 x 10.5 cm) • Pattern 6B • 3 cm wide strips from 5 different brown/green envelopes • Gold holographic paper • Figure scissors • Text sticker

Cut around the edge of the white card using the figure scissors. Cut out the bottle (not the top) and fill it with strips of envelope paper. Cut out the top from envelope paper (colour C) and stick it above the bottle. Stick everything on the red card. Pay attention: colour B stops after section 22!

Card 4
Card: brick red (Papicolor no. 33) (14.8 x 21 cm) and light grey (13.4 x 9.4 cm) • Pattern 6B • 3 cm wide strips from 5 different pink/ red envelopes • Gold holographic paper • Corner punch
Punch out the corners of the light grey card and follow the instructions given for card 3.

Card 5
Card: dark blue (14.8 x 21 cm) and rainbow blue (14 x 9.8 cm) • Pattern 6B • 3 cm strips from 5 different blue envelopes • Blue origami paper • Lily corner punch
Punch out the corners and follow the instructions given for card 3.

Card 6
Card: green (Papicolor no. 16) (14.8 x 21 cm) and rainbow beige (14.3 x 9 cm) • Pattern 6C • 2 cm wide strips from 4 different green and beige envelopes • Gold holographic paper • Cloud corner punch
Punch out the corners of the beige card. Cut out the bottom pan (not the handles) and fill it with the strips of envelope paper. Cut the other pans, the handles and the lid out of scrap pieces of envelope paper and stick them on the card according to the pattern.

pattern 6C

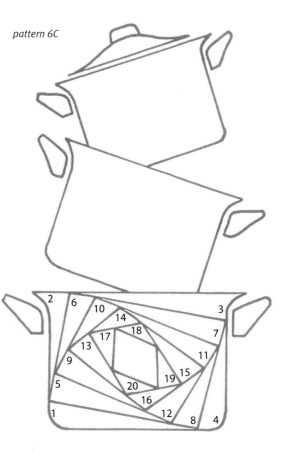

Card 7
Card: brick red (Papicolor no. 33) (14.8 x 21 cm and 14.4 x 10.1 cm) • Pattern 6C • 2 cm wide strips from 4 different grey envelopes • Silver holographic paper
Follow the instructions given for card 6.

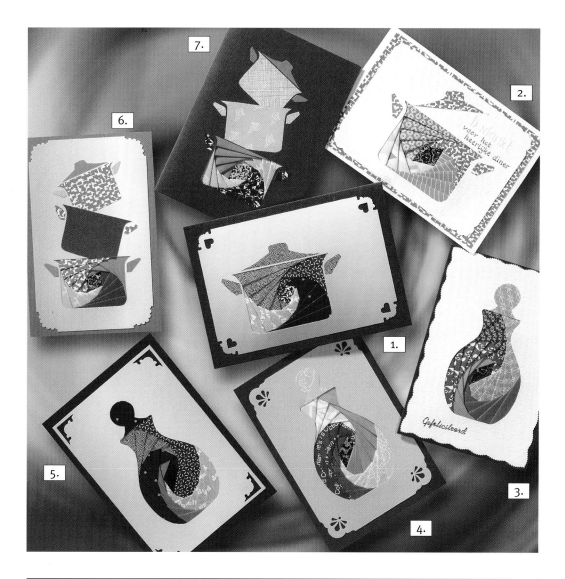

Windmills

The triangle, boat and windmill cards are all predominantly men's cards.

All the cards are made according to the instructions given for card 1.

Card 1

Card: lavender blue (Papicolor no. 31) (13.3 x 26.6 cm) and ecru (Papicolor no. 03) (12.2 x 12.2 cm) • Pattern 7 • 2 cm wide strips from 3 different blue envelopes • Silver holographic paper.

Carefully cut out the pattern's four large triangles. Fill the holes according to the instructions given for the basic triangle. Cut the four small triangles out of envelope paper (colour B) and stick them on the card according to the pattern.
Stick everything on the blue card.

Card 2

Card: lavender blue (Papicolor no. 31) (13.3 x 26.6 cm) and lilac (Papicolor no. 37) (12.5 x 12.5 cm) • Pattern 7 • 2 cm wide strips from 3 different blue envelopes • Silver holographic paper.

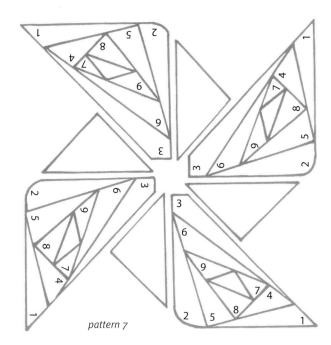

pattern 7

Card 3

Card: dark blue (Papicolor no. 41) (13.3 x 26.6 cm), light lavender (Papicolor no. 20) (12.6 x 12.6 cm), lavender (Papicolor no. 31) (12.4 x 12.4 cm) and cream (Papicolor no. 29) (12.4 x 12.4 cm) • Pattern 7 • 2 cm wide strips from 3 different blue envelopes • Figure scissors • Silver holographic paper
Cut around the edge of the cream card using the figure scissors.

Card 4

Card: white (13.3 x 26.6 cm and 13 x 13.3 cm) • Pattern 7 • 2 cm wide strips from 3 different blue envelopes • Red holographic paper

Card 5

Card: dark blue (13.3 x 26.6 cm and 13 x 13.3 cm) • Pattern 7 • 2 cm wide strips from 3 different blue/white envelopes • Silver holographic paper

Fluttering butterflies

Attractive cards which are suitable for using brightly coloured envelopes.

Cards 1 to 3 are made according to the instructions given for card 1. Cards 4 to 7 are made according to the instructions given for card 4.

Card 1
Card: dark blue (Papicolor no. 41) (13.3 x 26.6 cm) and white (11.8 x 11.8 cm) • Pattern 8A • 2 cm wide strips from 4 different blue envelopes • Butterfly corner punch • Silver holographic paper
Cut both wings out of the white card. Punch out the corners. Follow the instructions given for the basic triangle. Cut the body and the antennas out of a scrap piece of envelope paper and stick them on the card.

Card 2
Card: ecru (Papicolor no. 03) (13.3 x 26.6 cm) and blue (Papicolor no. 06) (13.3 x 13.3 cm)
• Pattern 8A • 2 cm wide strips from 4 different blue envelopes • Blue holographic paper.
Cut slanting corners on the front site of the ecru card as shown in the pattern on page 31. Once the wings have been filled, stick small pieces of double-sided adhesive tape on the inside of the ecru card on the left-hand side. Place the blue card exactly along the edge of the white card.

Card 3
Card: white (13.3 x 26.6 cm and 12.7 x 12.7 cm) and dark blue (12.7 x 12.7 cm) • Pattern 8A • 2 cm wide strips from 4 different blue envelopes • Silver holographic paper • Stickers
Cut slanting corners on the small white card.

Card 4
Card: lavender blue (Papicolor no. 31) (14.8 x 21 cm) and rainbow pink (14.6 x 9.5 cm) • Pattern 8B • 1.5 cm wide strips from 4 different pink, red, purple and blue envelopes • Heart corner punch • Fine-liner • Origami paper
Cut the four wings out of the rainbow card. Punch out the corners and fill the wings. Cut the bodies out of a scrap piece of blue paper and draw the antennas.

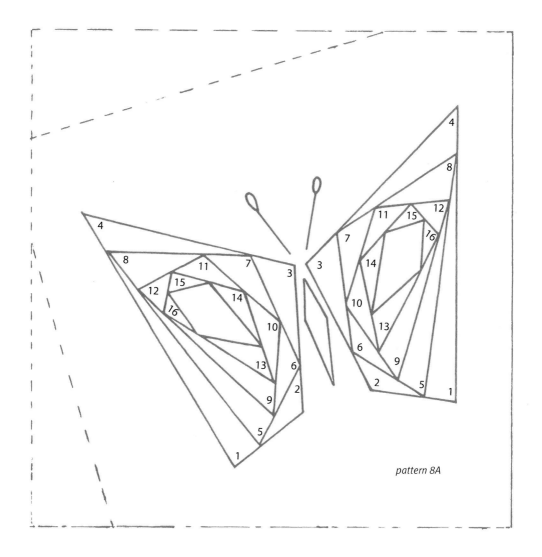

pattern 8A

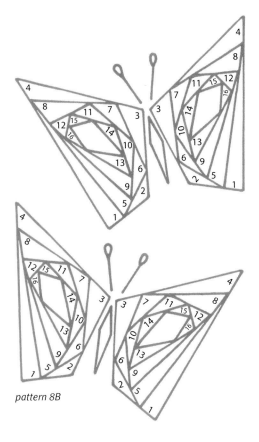

pattern 8B

Card 5

Card: pale blue (Papicolor no. 04) (14.8 x 21 cm) and dark green (Papicolor no. 18) (14.2 x 10.2 cm) • Pattern 8B • 1.5 cm wide strips from 4 different yellow/green envelopes • Gold holographic paper.

Cut slanting corners on the dark green card as shown in the photograph and fill the wings with strips of envelope paper. Give the butterflies a yellow body and antennas.

Card 6

Card: brick red (Papicolor no. 33) (14.8 x 21 cm) and rainbow orange (14.6 x 10.3 cm) • Pattern 8B • 1.5 cm wide strips from 4 different orange/ red envelopes • Gold holographic paper • Lily corner punch

Punch out the corners.

Card 7

Card: green (Papicolor no. 16) (14.8 x 21 cm and 14.4 x 10.1 cm) • Pattern 8B • 1.5 cm wide strips from 4 different beige/brown/light green envelopes • Silver holographic paper